A Basic Guide to Evaluation for Development Workers

**Frances
Rubin**

Oxfam
UK & Ireland

D0684268

Visual Basic .NET Class Design Handbook:
Coding Effective Classes

Visual Basic .NET Class Design Handbook: Coding Effective Classes

Author(s): Andy Olsen, Damon Allison, James Speer
ISBN: 1-861007-08-6
US$ 29.99
Can$ 46.99

Designing effective classes that you do not need to revisit and revise over and over again is an art. Within the .NET Framework, whatever code you write in Visual Basic .NET is encapsulated within the class hierarchy of the .NET Framework.

By investigating in depth the various members a class can contain, this handbook aims to give you a deep understanding of the implications of all the decisions you can make at design time. This book will equip you with the necessary knowledge to build classes that are robust, flexible, and reusable.

- **What you will learn from this book**
- The role of types in .NET
- The different kinds of type we can create in VB.NET
- How VB.NET defines type members
- The fundamental role of methods as containers of program logic
- The role of constructors and their effective use
- Object cleanup and disposal
- When and how to use properties and indexers to encapsulate data
- How .NET's event system works
- How to control and exploit inheritance in our types
- The logical and physical code organisation through namespaces and assemblies

Visual Basic .NET Text Manipulation Handbook:
String Handling and Regular Expressions

Author(s): François Liger, Craig McQueen, Paul Wilton
ISBN: 1-861007-30-2
US$ 29.99
Can$ 46.99

Text forms an integral part of many applications. Earlier version's of Visual
Basic would hide from you the intricacies of how text was being handled,
limiting your ability to control your program's execution or performance. The
.NET Framework gives you much finer control.

This handbook takes an in depth look at the text manipulation classes that
are included within the .NET Framework, in all cases providing you with
invaluable information as to their relative performance merits. The String and
Stringbuilder classes are investigated and the newly acquired support for regular expressions is illustrated in detail.

What you will learn from this book
- String representation and management within the .NET Framework
- Using the StringBuilder object to improve application performance
- Choosing between the different object's methods when manipulating text
- How to safely convert between String and other data types
- How to take advantage of .NET's Unicode representation of text for
  Internationalization
- The use of regular expressions including syntax and pattern matching to
  optimize your text manipulation operations

Visual Basic .NET Threading Handbook:

Author(s): K. Ardestani, F. C. Ferracchiati, S. Gopikrishna, T. Redkar, S. Sivakumar, T. Titus
ISBN: 1-861007-13-2
US$ 29.99
Can$ 46.99

All .NET languages now have access to the Free Threading Model that many Visual Basic Developers have been waiting for. Compared to the earlier apartment threading model, this gives you much finer control over where to implement threading and what you are given access to. It does also provide several new ways for your application to spin out of control.

This handbook explains how to avoid some common pitfalls when designing multi-threaded applications by presenting some guidelines for good design practice. By investigating .NET's threading model's architecture, you will be able to make sure that your applications take full advantage of it.

What you will learn from this book
- Thread creation
- Using timers to schedule threads to execute at specified intervals
- Synchronizing thread execution - avoiding deadlocks and race conditions
- Spinning threads from within threads, and synchronizing them
- Modelling your applications to a specific thread design model
- Scaling threaded applications by using the ThreadPool class
- Tracing your threaded application's execution in order to debug it

A catalogue record for this book is available from the British Library.

ISBN 0 85598 275 6

Available in Ireland from: Oxfam in Ireland, 19 Clanwilliam Terrace, Dublin 2. Telephone 01 6618544

Available in Canada and the United States of America from Westview Press, 5500 Central Avenue, Boulder, Colorado 80301, USA. Telephone (303) 4443541; Fax (303) 4493356

Published by Oxfam (UK and Ireland) 274 Banbury Road, Oxford, OX2 7DZ, UK.
Designed by Oxfam Design.
Printed by Oxfam Print Unit on environment-friendly paper.
Oxfam is a registered charity, no. 202918.

Acknowledgements

In 1992 I drafted the evaluation section of a proposed Oxfam procedures manual on project management. An adapted form has provided material for the *Oxfam Handbook for Development and Relief*, edited by Deborah Eade and Suzanne Williams. Some similarities may be found between this guide and parts of that text, as drafts have been swapped between us.

Particular thanks are due to Deborah Eade and Bridget Dillon, for comments, editing and friendship. Thanks, too, to Robert Nicholls for being a critical 'guinea-pig' at a particularly busy time.

This short guide to evaluation was originally intended for use within Oxfam but we hope that it will also be found helpful to a wider readership.

Contents

1 Introduction

There are many books on evaluation, some of them very interesting and helpful, others full of jargon and rather confusing. Oxfam staff who advise on planning and evaluation receive many requests for advice about different aspects of evaluation. The queries indicate a need for a simple guide that maps a route through the confusion that has built up around evaluation and its uses, that focuses on key underlying principles, and promotes clearer thinking.

A number of books and texts on evaluation have been drawn on in compiling this manual, in particular:

A UNICEF Guide for Monitoring and Evaluation: Making a Difference? UNICEF 1991.

Feuerstein, M T, *Partners in Evaluation*, Macmillan 1992

Beaudoux, E et al, *Supporting Development Action*, Macmillan 1992

Guide to Planning and Evaluating NGO Projects, Vols 1-3, NORAD

A workbook for implementing Partner Organisations and Support Agencies, AGKED/Misereor, 1991

Readers are advised to consult these books if they wish to study the subject in more detail. Other useful books are listed in the References and Further Reading section.

The manual is also based on the cumulative experience of staff in the advisory unit in doing evaluations, running workshops with field staff to discuss their evaluation experience, and advising staff about specific exercises; and on insights from colleagues in Oxfam, both in the UK and other countries.

1.1 Situations which might involve evaluation

Here are some examples of the situations that agency staff may experience in the course of their work which involve evaluation in some form:

• A grassroots or intermediary group may seek help on how to build evaluation into their work.

• A Northern funding agency may wish to encourage the building in of evaluation into the work of an organisation that is putting forward a proposal for funding.

• A Northern funding agency is not happy with the progress of an organisation that it is funding, or part-funding, and they wish to carry out an external evaluation.

• A major official donor wishes to do an evaluation of a group of projects that it is co-funding with a non-governmental agency. They have already appointed the evaluators and have only a limited amount of time in which to complete the exercise.

• Questions are asked about the effect of funding decisions taken over the years.

• Staff want to understand the effect of a particular policy they have been implementing, eg gender policy, disaster preparedness.

1.2 Questions about evaluation

Here are some examples of the questions most often asked about evaluation:

• How do we draw up terms of reference (TOR)?

• We want the evaluation to be as participative as possible, do you have any tips?

• How can we reconcile partner agency needs and the funding agency needs?

• What indicators should we use?

- What is the appropriate method?

- Should it be qualitative or quantitative?

- Who should do the evaluation?

- What is an acceptable cost?

- When is it best to evaluate, and how long does it take?

- We've had awful problems with external evaluators so we've decided just to promote internal evaluations — how do we go about it?

1.3 The aim of the guide, and what it covers

This guide is intended to help people to understand the underlying principles of evaluation, in order to be clearer about its uses and limitations. It will deal with questions such as what evaluation actually is and why it is useful; when it is inappropriate; how to develop programmes and projects that can be effectively evaluated; the steps necessary for planning an evaluation; and how to use evaluation to improve development action. It will emphasise the dangers in not being clear about why an evaluation is being requested; the need to involve people; the political nature of evaluation and the importance of negotiation.

The second chapter of the guide puts evaluation in context. Evaluation is defined, and then its place in projects is discussed. There is also a discussion on its relationship to planning, appraisal and monitoring.

There are different 'actors' involved in development, and these different actors may have very different views on things. For this reason negotiation is important at all the various stages in a development initiative, not least when considering evaluation.

A brief history of 'traditional' evaluation and its characteristics is given in Chapter 3. There is a discussion on why NGOs need to reassess evaluation, and the alternative options available. This is followed by a section on the political nature of evaluation, and issues of power and control.

Chapter 4 looks at why people do evaluation, and what evaluation can and cannot do. Chapter 5 outlines the main questions that have to be addressed when evaluation is incorporated at an early stage in project planning.

The next chapter considers practical considerations when planning a specific evaluation exercise. There is advice on drawing up terms of reference, and ensuring better feedback and follow up, including suggestions on presenting evaluation reports. The final part of the chapter covers particular points that evaluators need to consider.

The last chapter looks at the important questions of feedback and use of the findings of an evaluation.

There are appendices with checklists of questions, and an explanation of the terms used in the manual are given in a glossary. There is also an annotated bibliography of the most helpful and accessible books on evaluation.

2 Putting evaluation in context

2.1 Evaluation in the project cycle

Evaluation means 'to assess the value or worth of'. For our purposes we broaden this out to mean 'to understand the value of something in order to do things better in the future'.

This guide will focus on evaluation activity related to development projects. The points covered can also apply to evaluations of emergency work, particularly if emergencies are understood from a development perspective. Because 'project' is still the most widely-used term to describe development activities, it will be used in this guide, although it is rather a limited way of describing development.

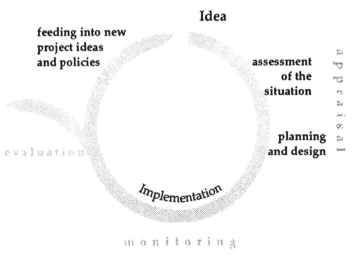

The project cycle

The project cycle is a useful way of describing how development ideas turn into a proposal for action. As the proposal is implemented, it should be dynamic and flexible enough to change in the light of lessons learnt; evaluation is one of the most valuable tools for learning.

The diagram on the previous page does not take full account of the complex nature of development work, and the interactions between the different people involved. Each stage should be the occasion of learning and change, and perhaps a spiral rather than a circle would be a better representation of the way the development process builds on past experience. The diagram also shows that evaluation may sometimes not be used, and evaluation reports may lie unread on dusty shelves.

This book is intended to help readers to make full use of evaluations.

2.2 Appraisal, monitoring and evaluation

A distinction is usually made between appraisal, monitoring and evaluation.

• Appraisal is the critical examination of a proposal, on the basis of agreed selection criteria, before implementation or approval for funding.

The appraisal phase will involve asking questions such as:

• How has the problem to be addressed been identified?

• Does the proposed action address the problem?

• Do the people proposing to carry out the work have the capacity to do it?

• Which different interest groups have been involved in defining the problem and choosing the course of action?

• How are different groups of men and women likely to be incorporated or affected by the project (young/old, landed/ landless, single-headed households)?

• Monitoring is a continuous, methodical process of data collection and information-gathering throughout the life of a project. The information collected can be used for regular evaluation of progress, so that adjustments can be made while the work is going on.
Monitoring is also used to mean the systematic 'tracking' of a particular condition, or set of conditions (for example political events, environmental change, the situation of women), to identify trends.

• Evaluation is a learning and management tool: an assessment of what has taken place in order to improve future work. Measuring, analysing and interpreting change helps people to determine how far objectives have been achieved and whether the initial assumptions about what would happen were right; and to make judgements about the effectiveness, efficiency, impact and sustainability of the work.

2.3 The relationship between appraisal, monitoring and evaluation

2.3.1 Appraisal

A proposal for a new project should state clearly the objectives and activities, and the resources required. The assumptions on which the project is based should also be explained, and there should be some indication of how progress will be measured. Time and thought given, at the initial planning stage, to the way in which monitoring and evaluation will be built into the work, will create the conditions for the success of the project, and make it more 'evaluable'. Projects should start on a sound basis of information, especially a knowledge of the roles, responsibilities and requirements of women and men in a community, and within the project.

Everyone who has an interest in a particular project, the 'stakeholders' (funder, local NGO, and the women and men involved directly in the work), should identify and agree on the criteria for assessing the progress of the project. They should jointly select the indicators which will show that change has taken place. During the life of a project, it is quite possible, and may even be desirable, that criteria and indicators should evolve in response to experience gained and changing objectives. Indicators should provide relevant information, of value to those who will use the findings, and there should be a balance between quantitative and qualitative indicators (see p. 40). It is a poor use of resources to collect too much data, of poor quality or little relevance, and generally frustrating for those involved in collecting it.

The appraisal stage of a project should also involve the consideration of different options for addressing the problem. This is the point at which monitoring and evaluation expectations of the different parties involved will be negotiated.

2.3.2 Monitoring

In monitoring, information for 'tracking' progress against previously agreed plans and 'milestones' is routinely gathered. The changes that are resulting from project activities can be identified: both the effects and the impact (see p. 38). If there are discrepancies between actual and planned progress, corrective action can be taken. This can include changing the overall purpose and plan of the activity. Monitoring can also mean keeping a check on the use of resources. Questions for later evaluation can be identified during monitoring.

2.3.3 Evaluation

Evaluation uses information gathered during regular monitoring, but may need other information as well. It often uses 'baseline information': information collected at the very beginning of a project, against which progress can be measured. Evaluation happens at set times in the life of a project.

Evaluation looks at the relevance, effectiveness and impact of a project, with the aim of improving an existing project or influencing future policies, programmes and projects.

2.3.4 Appraisal, monitoring and evaluation in the project cycle

In terms of timing within the project cycle, and basic purpose, monitoring and evaluation are distinct from appraisal, but all three can use similar approaches and methods for gathering and analysing information.

Although monitoring and evaluation are different processes, there are times when they merge. If monitoring systems work well, evaluation is necessary less often, and when it is necessary, it is easier to carry out.

Monitoring and evaluation are only tools to help in development. If it looks as if plans should be modified, do not wait for the end of a project or for a planned evaluation. The success of a project may depend on its ability to change dynamically when necessary.

2.4 The stakeholders in development action

There are many different people with an interest in development projects. It is important to identify these stakeholders, their needs, motives, and interests, and the relations between them. In turn, they operate within their own wider environments, each with a different set of stakeholders.

The way in which the different development stakeholders relate to each other determines the type of partnership that develops within a project. It is important to identify the different expectations that people may have about these relationships. If this is not done it can lead to conflict, uncertainty, and a breakdown in communications. This is true of all stages of project work: planning, implementation and evaluation.

The values, principles and objectives held by different people may appear to be the same, but each person may be interpreting them differently, and have different priorities and approaches. This is why negotiation between development partners about objectives and activities is so important. Objectives should be reviewed at regular intervals by everyone involved. Are they still relevant and appropriate in the light of experience?

The 'target group', or the men and women who are to be the prime beneficiaries of a project, should be the most important stakeholders. It is still rare for them to participate fully in the definition of development action and the planning of projects. There is increasing evidence that the more people are enabled to participate in decisions about development activities which affect them, the more successful and sustainable the activities will be.

The most important questions for the target group are:

• Does the project tackle their real needs?

• Are the results significant?

• Are the results worth the effort?

The answers are likely to be different for men and women.

Apart from the 'partners' in development action, described above, there are other groups to relate to at the regional and national level: for example, national and local government authorities, labour unions, development assistance agencies, other organised groups. Even if they are not directly involved in the project, they may have opinions about it. It is important to find out their views and work out ways of relating to them.

Organisations which provide funding do so on condition that the assistance they give is in line with their overall policies. They are accountable to boards of management, public opinion, and supporters, and control is often a major concern for them. They have to spend their funds according to the agreements made, and they need to be sure that projects achieve the intended objectives.

The different stakeholders will try to influence the choice of objectives, priorities, and methods for projects according to their own values and principles. At times this can cause conflict and power struggles, particularly when a donor organisation's influence predominates because of their control of financial resources.

Planning and evaluation of projects should be based on an acknowledgement of possible conflicting motives and interests, or these activities may become nothing more than theoretical exercises, dominated by the stronger (funding) partner. The interests of the 'target' groups'should have the highest priority, in practice as well as intent.

3 Traditional and alternative models of evaluation

3.1 Traditional evaluation

Historically many evaluation ideas and methods developed as a result of the need to understand how money was being spent on social and education programmes in the West, in order to justify expenditure to funders. During the Second World War, 1939-45, attempts were made to carry out formal evaluations of military training. There was also a growing interest in the observation and recording of the way people behaved in different contexts, and the development of systems for the statistical measurement of beliefs and attitudes.

Concepts of evaluation related to development came into being in response to the requirements of large-scale government and bilateral agencies to see clear management and control in projects, which were focused on capital-intensive growth and technology transfer. This explains the predominance of economics and cost-benefit analysis in the 1960s and 1970s, and the view that development is something essentially tangible and measurable. Within this view of development, evaluation is seen as a means of control, focusing on predetermined aims in as objective a way as possible. This approach relies heavily on the measurement of quantitative data (numbers of things that can be counted) with only minimal allowance for qualitative aspects (less tangible aspects of development that need to be described through views and words).

This type of evaluation, which is often referred to as 'traditional', has the following characteristics:

1 A search for objectivity and a 'scientific approach', through standardised procedures. The values used in this approach, rather than being truly objective, often reflect the priorities of the evaluator, and an underlying Western world view.

2 An over-reliance on quantitative measures. Qualitative aspects of development, being difficult to measure, tend to be ignored.

3 A high degree of managerial control, whereby managers can influence the questions being asked. (They usually ensure that they are left out of what is to be evaluated!) Other people, who may be affected by the findings of an evaluation, may have little input, either in shaping the questions to be asked or reflecting on the findings.

4 Outsiders are usually contracted to be evaluators in the belief that this will increase objectivity, and there may be a negative perception of them by those 'being evaluated'.

(These ideas are drawn from an unpublished dissertation submitted for an MA thesis to the London School of Economics in 1991 by Joanna Rowlands, 'How do we know it's working?The evaluation of social development projects'.)

At first, traditional evaluation approaches and methods were adopted by non-governmental organisations (NGOs) involved in development, but over the years they have often been found inappropriate in terms of scale, cost, and the underlying technocratic view of development. Resistance to evaluation has built up in response to inappropriate use of these methods.

While evaluation is essentially a tool to help in development, it can be a highly-charged process politically, because of the relations of power and control that exist between funder and funded, between implementing agency and target population, between management and staff, and so on.

For example, Northern-based funding NGOs have often had poor information systems, and they have tended to call for evaluations to fill information gaps, or as a response to a sudden recognition that an organisation or project is in crisis. The effect has been especially negative where evaluation has been linked to funding decisions.

In such a context, evaluations have too often seemed like one-sided interrogations by funders, and have been of limited use, because those carrying out a project have felt little involvement in or ownership of the exercise. It is not surprising that staff and members of organisations subjected to such evaluations should feel insecure and unco-operative.

3.2 Reassessment of evaluation: the challenge for NGOs

Today, NGOs, both funded and funders, face a challenge that demands re-assessment of evaluation and its potential uses. Increasingly NGOs have been praised as effective agents for the encouragement of grassroots development, and for their ability to reach poor women and men, at lower cost. There has been an increase in funds from multilateral and bilateral agencies to NGOs, and it seems likely that these agencies will wish to channel even more through Northern NGOs and directly to Southern NGOs in future.

However, NGOs have been unable to provide firm evidence about the results of development efforts, since few, if any, have produced accessible information, based on systematic evaluation of projects and programmes. In addition, there is a growing scepticism on the part of the tax-paying and donating public about the results of development aid.

NGOs need to be able to prove that they are effective. They must develop their ability to evaluate their work, in order to demonstrate the positive change their efforts are helping to bring about; and to use the results of evaluation to learn how to improve their work.

3.3 Ideas about development and the role of evaluation

As discussed above, the traditional model of evaluation was developed in response to a technocratic view of development, where development inputs could be measured in numbers.

Today, many NGOs think of development more in terms of people than of things, of enabling poor and disadvantaged women and men to have more say in ensuring their livelihoods, and shaping their societies: development is seen to be more about social change than technocratic solutions; and partnership, participation and the dignity of people are valued. Evaluation should be integral to the development process, and it is important to find ways of evaluating that match this perception of development. Also, if the people carrying out project activities are more involved in evaluating them, they are much more likely to use the results of that evaluation in present or future work.

3.4 Alternative approaches to evaluation

Over the last two decades various alternatives to the traditional forms of evaluation have developed. These approaches can make use of some of the tools used in traditional evaluation, but the aim is to make them more appropriate to measuring social development.

Traditional evaluation tends to see the people involved in a project as objects of an evaluation; alternative approaches take the view that participants in development projects should be the 'subjects' of evaluation and take a more active role. The methods chosen should enhance their capacity to collect and analyse information relevant to them and their situation.

Alternative approaches owe much to developments in Latin America and Asia in the 1970s and 1980s. They are characterised by:

• A view of evaluation as an integral part of the development or change process: 'reflection-action'.

• An understanding of evaluation as an 'empowering process', rather than control by an external body.

• A recognition of subjectivity in evaluation.

• A recognition that different groups of men and women will have different perceptions, which are equally valid. There is a need for negotiation during the process of evaluation, to reach consensus about conclusions and recommendations.

• A tendency to use less formal techniques such as unstructured interviews, and participant observation.

• An emphasis on sociological enquiry rather than economic measurements.

• The evaluator taking on the role of facilitator, rather than being an objective and neutral outsider.

(These ideas are also drawn from the MA dissertation by Joanna Rowlands, 'How do we know it's working? The evaluation of social development projects', referred to above.)

3.5 Power and control

Power and control are central issues in evaluation. Traditional methods of evaluation enabled funding NGOs to control the use of their funds for development activities. But if the aim is to increase the control which the women and men who are taking part in a project have over its progress, then the alternative approach to evaluation is more appropriate. Both funding and implementing NGOs need to use a range of methods for evaluation that will provide the information necessary, and also encourage critical reflection by all those involved. In particular, Northern funding NGOs must be willing to carry out the same kind of critical reflection about their own activities and approach as they demand of those NGOs they fund.

There is a need for greater clarity between all the parties involved regarding how, by whom, and against what criteria, work is going to be measured. This is one way of building more honest relations among development actors. The tensions that underlie much evaluation work relate to:

• A lack of recognition and open discussion of issues of power and control.

• A lack of open discussion and negotiation about different perceptions of development work, and the function of evaluation within this: whether it is a control mechanism or a creative tool to enhance people's critical capacity to change their situation.

• Different perceptions of what is 'successful'.

- A misuse of evaluation: to fudge decision-taking, for example.
- Cultural differences in ways of working and expressing things.

Evaluation will work best where it is understood as an integral part of development work, and where there is an environment which encourages critical reflection. Otherwise people can feel insecure about their role and jobs. Morale can be affected by adverse findings, that are insensitively communicated. Much depends on where the decision to initiate evaluation comes from, and how the results are used.

Staff of funding NGOs should be encouraged to take an active interest in upgrading their knowledge and skills, to enable them to engage confidently in evaluation work, and to advise counterparts.

4 The purpose and use of evaluation

4.1 Reasons for evaluation

There are many different reasons why evaluations are carried out. Some good reasons are to measure progress and effectiveness; to look at costs and efficient use of resources; to find out if it is necessary to change the way things are being done; and to learn from what has happened in order to make plans for the future. These are all constructive reasons, within the control of those organising their work.

There are other, less good, reasons why evaluations are carried out. An evaluation might be demanded by a funding agency, who are wondering whether to go on supporting a project; or there might be a statutory requirement for evaluation from a government department. Evaluations are sometimes done as part of a research project as a way of testing out new techniques for gathering information; or sometimes because people who raise funds for an organisation need something to put in their publicity material. Evaluations may be done routinely, as a matter of policy at some high level of the organisation, without anyone being very clear about why they are done. Evaluations done for some of these reasons are likely to be seen by those most directly involved in the work under scrutiny as being imposed from outside. The people who are taking part in the activities being evaluated are probably not fully informed in advance, and have little say in the matter of what is evaluated and how. They will seldom be told about the results of the evaluation.

Sometimes, expensive and disruptive evaluations have been carried out by funders when decisions have already been made about whether or not to continue financial support. Evaluations can be used as excuses for getting rid of certain staff, when what was needed was a management review. Where there is a suspicion of serious misconduct within an organisation, it is better to do an audit than an evaluation. Evaluation can be misused, to cover up weaknesses in a programme by only focusing on what is 'good'. Conflicting groups within a project or organisation may demand an evaluation, when what is really needed is a facilitator to deal with the conflict, after which an evaluation should be a more constructive process.

If used well evaluation can contribute to development action, but it cannot solve every problem, or answer every question. Above all, evaluation cannot be a substitute for good management and firm decision making; it can only provide information to help in these processes.

4.2 Judging success and failure

Sometimes evaluations are expected to show clearly whether or not a project has been 'successful'. It is often very difficult to show clear evidence of success, because this may depend on so many factors, some of which are beyond the control of the project. It is often easier to show failure, and unfortunately, evaluations often concentrate on this. Another problem is that different groups of people will have different perceptions about what constitutes failure and success. The time-scale can also be a factor: a project may be deemed a failure at one stage, but several years later it may become clear that there were some positive effects. A failure may well spark off other activities that lead to positive change.

4.3 Measuring quantity and quality

Evaluation is concerned with measurements. Evaluators will almost certainly want to know details of costs, and the quantities of resources that the project uses. Many of the inputs which a project uses (salaries, materials, tools, petrol) are measurable. Evaluators will also want to assess the activities that have taken place, and the changes that have resulted from project efforts, and want to know how many people are involved, and the products or services which the project generates. These may sometimes be very obviously measurable in terms of numbers: acreage cultivated, vaccinations carried out, springs protected. Whatever can be expressed in terms of numbers, amounts, and quantities are termed the quantitative aspects of evaluation.

Of course, not all the inputs or changes are measurable in this way. How do you measure advice given, or level of self-confidence achieved? Evaluators must be very careful that they do not just concentrate on what can be easily counted, but must be sure they take account of the uncountable factors too: such things as beliefs and attitudes, level of knowledge or skill, behaviour, and motivation. These qualitative factors may be extremely important in determining whether projects are successful or not.

It is often what people think about a programme which is the really significant factor in their level of involvement and commitment to it, and therefore whether it achieves its objectives or not. In order to find out why a programme has followed a certain course, it is vital to look at the programme as a whole. It is not enough to know that a programme has succeeded or failed: it is even more important to know why. That means taking account of all the unmeasurable factors as well as the things that can be counted.

4.4 What evaluation can do

1 Evaluation can improve the management of programmes and projects and related activities, and point to the better usage of funds and other resources.

2 Evaluation can help people to learn from experience so as to improve the relevance, methods, and results of projects and programmes, for current and future work.

3 Evaluation can increase accountability:

• to donors: to meet their demands that resources are being used effectively, efficiently and for agreed objectives;

• of donors to the organisations they fund and work with;

- to the men and women in whose name these organisations are working.

4 Evaluation can provide information to enhance communications, within projects and organisations, and between different stakeholders, and also for advocacy work.

4.5 What evaluation can not and should not be used for

1 Evaluation is not decision-making, but can only provide information for decision-makers.

2 Evaluation should not be used to protect managers from the need to face difficult decisions.

3 Evaluation should not be used for crisis management.

5 Putting evaluation into practice

5.1 Developing evaluable projects and programmes

The aim of this guide is not only to explain what evaluation can and cannot do, but to help people to make sure that when evaluation is carried out, it is useful, and lessons can be learned from it.

Evaluation reports often say that 'it was difficult or practically impossible to do a "proper" evaluation'. The usual complaint is that there is no statement of how things were at the start of a project, no idea given as to what kind of changes were hoped for, or what indicators could be used to measure change. If information has not been collected during the project, it is difficult to trace changes in direction, or measure achievements. Occasionally evaluators complain of an overload of unfocused information.

Remember that evaluation is a tool for learning and better management. The aim is to assess what has taken place in order to improve future work. Evaluation needs to be thought about, discussed and negotiated from the very early stages of a project because:

- It can be a highly sensitive event, often bringing together people with different agendas.

- It depends on information generated at several stages of a project.

5.2 The key questions

Asking a few key questions during the appraisal and planning stage of a project will help to make evaluation an integral part of the design and methodology of the project, and to plan for future information needs.

1 **Why and for whom:** the purpose of the evaluation; why is it being done, and who is asking for it?

2 **When:** the timing of the evaluation; at what point in the life of the project or programme will it take place?

3 **What:** what is the scope and focus of the evaluation; what will it look at, what are the key questions to answer?

4 **Who:** who is responsible for managing the exercise, who is going to carry it out (do the evaluating)?

5 **How:** how is the exercise to be carried out, how will information be gathered; how long will it take; what criteria and indicators will be used?

6 **How much:** what resources will be needed, financial and other?

7 **What then:** how will findings be reported and to whom; how will findings be shared and presented to different audiences; what is the procedure for follow up?

These questions should be asked when considering a project proposal for funding, or deciding how best to organise an operational project. In the case of funded work, it will be important to distinguish between monitoring and evaluation that are internal to the organisation of the project, and that which relates to expectations or agreements with the funders or sponsors. A funding NGO must be explicit about how it is going to judge a partner organisation's performance over time, and what its expectations are in terms of evaluation. It is equally important that an NGO, when receiving funds, is clear about what commitments it is making to a particular organisation, and how its own performance will be judged. These expectations should be the subject of negotiations when financial and other support is discussed.

Each question will now be looked at in more detail.

5.3 Why and for whom is an evaluation to be done?

5.3.1 *Why is the evaluation being done?*

The reasons for doing evaluations can be grouped as follows:

i To improve performance
This is 'formative' evaluation, helping to 'form' or shape work while it is still going on. This kind of evaluation is useful for those directly involved in, or in charge of work. It can identify problems, and things that are working well and can be built on. It can also check whether or not objectives have evolved, and be a way of keeping the different people involved in the project informed about progress or the need for change.

ii To make choices and decisions
This is 'summative' evaluation, a summing-up of a project to make a judgement of how effective it has been in achieving results. Information from such evaluations can be used to compare different ways of doing things, to help people make choices between types of development action. This kind of evaluation can be used by funders to decide on whether to continue support or not.

iii To learn lessons
The prime purpose of an evaluation may be learning, so that the results can be shared within a project, between projects, between organisations and so on. For example, a funding NGO may evaluate a variety of work with a particular sector of the population, to see which approaches have the best results, and why.

iv To increase accountability
Evaluations may be a condition of receiving funds, as donors want to be sure that their funds are being used effectively. They may also want to find out if there are alternative ways of doing the work.

Evaluations to promote accountability of donors and implementing agencies to the women and men they are supporting are rare. Improving the way evaluations are set up can encourage greater two-way accountability.

An evaluation may have more than one purpose, but it is important for stakeholders to agree on the priority purposes. This can help to limit the scope of an evaluation and make it more manageable. Identifying stakeholders, and making sure that they agree about the main purpose of an evaluation, is essential in order to decide on the approach and methods to be used in actually carrying it out.

5.3.2 Who wants the evaluation?

There are different people who might want an evaluation done. The people who have an interest in the work being evaluated, the 'stakeholders', could be:

- those involved in managing and carrying out a project
- the women and men targeted/taking part in a project
- funding agencies
- major co-funders eg EEC/ODA
- advisory units in an agency
- individuals in organisations carrying out similar work
- government departments
- policy makers.

Stakeholders need to be clear about what they expect from an evaluation. The process of negotiating the purpose of an evaluation is very important, and time should be spent on this. It may not be possible to reconcile the wishes of all stakeholders, and skill is needed in managing evaluation processes to deal with tensions that might occur.

5.4 When should the evaluation take place?

Evaluation should happen at regular intervals in the life of a project, to build up a clear picture of progress and impact. The type of programme will affect timing. For example, if objectives are long-term it may be two years before any useful assessment of progress can be made. A short-term intervention will need to have an evaluation done immediately, to look at how it was carried out, and the results. If the longer-term impact of a project is important, evaluation will have to happen some time after the project is finished.

5.4.1 When, in the life of a project, should evaluation take place?

Gathering information for monitoring and on-going evaluation should be built into project work as a continuous process. But there are special times in the project's life when more organised 'stand back' evaluations take place:

i. Appraisal or ex-ante evaluation
Information collected before a project starts, or in the very early stages, helps to define what is to be done, and provides a baseline from which to measure change.

ii. On-going evaluation
Monitoring indicates whether activities are being carried out as planned and what changes are happening as a result. Monitoring should be accompanied by on-going evaluation, which analyses the information in order to improve performance during a project. If a project has been conducting regular on-going evaluation, and this is well-documented, more formal evaluations may be unnecessary.

iii. Mid-term evaluation
This may be timed to take place after a particular stage of a project, to see what has happened so far, and make adjustments for the next stage, particularly when activities are planned to go on for two years or more. This kind of evaluation tends to concentrate on management and the balance of inputs and outputs. Donors may sometimes make payments for a second year conditional on a mid-

term evaluation. An annual report, written by a project manager, can be a useful evaluative document.

iv. Final evaluation
This will happen at the end of a project, in order to learn lessons about how the project has been implemented and the results. A final report of a project written by a project manager can be evaluative, comparing objectives with what was achieved.

v. Ex-post evaluations
These happen some time (often two years or more) after a project has finished. They look at impact and sustainability. They also consider broader 'policy' issues. This kind of evaluation is rare in NGOs, and more effort should be put into promoting such studies.

5.4.2 Other times when evaluations take place

An evaluation may be called for when:

i A problem is identified by monitoring or on-going evaluation, and it is decided to investigate further.

ii. A donor, for example a major co-funder, may request an evaluation to fit in with their own institutional requirements.

iii. An organisation decides it wants to look at a particular aspect of work, maybe in relation to areas identified in its programme plan.

5.4.3 Other important factors relating to timing

There are other time-related factors to consider at an early stage, particularly when planning a large and expensive evaluation, that involves a lot of different people:

i. Climate, seasons and key events in the calendar

• When are the key religious festivals? When do people have other commitments? When might it be inappropriate to do field work, or schedule meetings?

• What political events can be foreseen, eg elections, party congresses?

• What are the busy times in the year for organisations and projects and government departments, eg end of the financial year.

• Are there times in the year when access to particular project areas is impossible? Or when it is so hot that people will have difficulty concentrating in discussion sessions?

• Are there significant patterns of work over the year? There may be periods when there are few men around, because they have migrated for work. The women left behind may have little time to spare for evaluation sessions.

• When are the harvest and 'lean' periods? How do they affect women and men and their capacity to engage in an evaluation?

ii. Use of people's time, or opportunity cost
• Do project staff and beneficiaries feel there will be a benefit to them in participating in an evaluation exercise, even though they have plenty of other things to do?

• Are there some days when people are especially busy? Are there significant differences between men and women's timetables?

• Are particular interest groups unavailable at certain times?

iii. The availability of external evaluators
If people from outside the project/organisation are going to be involved, they may well be in demand, and only available during specific periods.

iv. The length of time the evaluation will take
Regular on-going evaluation may only involve project staff in a couple of days every month or every few months. Formal evaluations will need several months of preparation (but should not last beyond one year, because there is a risk of losing continuity if people change their jobs). The time will depend on what information is available or needs to be prepared, and how many weeks of field work are necessary. When the evaluation has been done, several weeks or months may be needed to study the results, prepare the report, and discuss it with those involved. The amount of time needed for more formal exercises should not be under-estimated. It is important to plan this into work.

Field visits need to be long enough to enable the collection of necessary information and should avoid the 'fly in-fly out' style of development. Discussion time should not be forfeited to endless journeys to make a fleeting visit to the most far-flung group. The more actively involved the women and men who participate in a project are in the evaluation, the longer the exercise is likely to take.

5.5 What is the scope and focus of the evaluation?

Three sets of questions should be built into any evaluation:

• What changes have taken place, and are these changes the ones which the original plan hoped for? Evaluations should give an account of what the project has achieved, or not achieved, and compare this with expectations.

• What were the reasons for the success or failure? It is important to know why things happened as they did, and analyse the factors which influenced the way the project progressed.

• What actions should now be taken? Evaluators should suggest courses of action, in the light of answers to the first two questions.

5.5.1 The focus of an evaluation

At the planning stage of a project decisions can be made about what to focus on in particular evaluations. The focus might be:

• a geographic area

• groups of beneficiaries

• types of activities

• time period

• a particular kind of activity over a group of projects to compare effectiveness (a thematic evaluation)

• a group of projects all working in the same area to see how they interact with each other.

Some projects may be so small that such divisions are inappropriate. Nearer the time of preparing for the actual evaluation, it will be necessary to review, and possibly to change, the focus. If monitoring and evaluation are taking place within projects, this information can be gathered together for a thematic evaluation. This is one way of making resources spent on evaluation go further. It also helps to build up a picture to enable evaluation of overall programmes.

There are a number of 'levels of interaction' which could be the focus for an evaluation: the funding NGO's relationship to the project, or the implementing agency; or agency relationships with project participants.

Sometimes it may be appropriate to have a much narrower focus. For example, those in charge of a project may be aware of a problem but not sure exactly what it is. A 'process' evaluation may be carried out which will look at how a project is functioning, and its management.

In some instances an evaluation is not appropriate. If there are serious doubts about a particular project, then a project audit might be in order. An audit will examine whether a project conforms with required policies and procedures, and whether resources are being used as planned.

5.5.2 What is the role of the funder in an evaluation?

The interests of the funder may dominate the evaluation process, given its relative power. If an NGO is a sole funder, it may wish to evaluate the whole of the project. If it is only funding part of a project, it may only feel able to evaluate that particular aspect of the work. In this case it may be worthwhile to involving all the funders in an evaluation, so that donors' demands are coordinated, resources are pooled, and they gain a shared understanding of the work.

However important the role of the funders, the implementing organisation must also be able to state its views.

5.5.3 What criteria should be used for evaluation?

The criteria that are commonly used as a focus for shaping evaluation questions are:

i. Effectiveness: how far is the project or programme achieving objectives? For example, the project might be concerned with the training of primary health care workers to improve their technical skills, or disseminating information about sustainable agricultural practices. Achievements at this level are project outputs, or what was done. The inputs are the human, financial and material resources that were provided, to achieve the objectives.

ii. Efficiency: what is the cost of achieving the objectives?
A project may be very 'effective' in working towards its objectives, but it may be doing so at very high cost (both socially and economically), which is neither replicable or sustainable. There may be ways of achieving the same things more cheaply. This may involve looking at how things are organised, what type of technology is being employed, as well as financial management.

iii. Relevance: is the project relevant?
A project may or may not prove to be appropriate to the needs of the women and men it is designed to help. There might be other problems that should take priority. The overall approach and strategy of the project should be consistent with the problem and intended effects.

iv.Impact: what are the effects of the project?
The impact of a project is the social, economic, technical, environmental and other effects on individual men and women, and communities directly or indirectly involved in the project. The impact on women and on men may be different. Part of the impact may have been changes in the institutions involved. The number of people affected should be estimated.

Impacts can be intended and unintended, positive and negative, immediate or long-term. They can operate at the micro level (for example, at household level) or macro level (they may affect a whole sector).

Sometimes a distinction is made between shorter-term results (outcomes) and longer-term results (impacts). For example, outcomes could be a change in the way people do things as a result of the project, e.g. domestic servants may no longer be prepared to work for less than minimum wages. However, if the overall impact hoped for is an improvement in standard of living, and basic health, through improved income and conditions, it could be very difficult to prove the causality between the intervention of a small project and what actually happens. So many other external influences can have an effect.

v. Sustainability: will project activities and benefits continue after external support is withdrawn?

Many types of work cannot be financially self-sustaining. The issue is how far the men and women directly involved can take charge themselves of finding the resources necessary. There are two key aspects of sustainability for social development programmes: social/institutional and economic.

Another aspect of sustainability is the effect the project has on the environment and natural resources.

vi. Progress: is the project achieving the original objectives, or have these changed?

An evaluation can also question the objectives and design of the project itself. It may be concluded that a project is progressing very well, even though it is far from meeting the original objectives. These may have been too ambitious, or irrelevant. The evaluation may also look at who was involved in setting objectives: was it only project leaders or were staff and beneficiaries also involved?

5.5.4 Who chooses the criteria?

Different people involved in a project may have different perceptions of what is 'success'. Funders and funded should be open about the criteria that each will use for determining change and progress, and how these criteria will be translated into indicators relevant to a particular situation. Project organisers should also be allowed to state how they will judge their own work, given what they say they are setting out to do.

Much more work needs to be done to enable the women and

men at the grassroots level to be able to state what 'measures' they will use to judge the progress of projects designed to benefit them.

5.5.5 What indicators should be used?

Indicators, which show that change has taken place, are of different sorts. Indicators can be used simply to track what is being done, and how; these are termed 'process indicators'. They will tend to focus at the level of inputs and outputs, monitoring the use of resources and recording the activities being carried out. 'Impact indicators' indicators; impactrefer to those indicators that show whether the project efforts are having any effect, whether any changes have taken place as a result of the project activities. This type of indicator can show the extent to which project objectives are being met, and if there is progress towards overall aims.

Indicators can be quantitative, concerned with numbers or amounts, for example, the child mortality rate, the incidence of disease in a particular community; or qualitative, concerned with descriptions and attitudes, and with what people feel they can achieve as the result of a project. To look at qualitative indicators, qualitative methods and techniques of information gathering will probably be necessary.

5.5.7 When should indicators be chosen and who should choose them?

Ideally, indicators should be identified at the outset of a project. The careful thought required to define what indicators will be evidence of progress and change in line with objectives can be salutary. If indicators are identified at the start, then information about them can be collected as part of the regular activities of the project.

It is useful to select both quantitative and qualitative indicators. Just because quantitative indicators are easier to measure, for example, number of courses held, numbers of people attending each training, they should not dominate. Quantitative information needs qualifying with information about why people attend courses or not, and how they are using what they have learnt.

There is often a temptation to define long lists of indicators at the planning stage of a project, and then to find that collecting information becomes so burdensome that it is abandoned. It is better to concentrate on the really significant factors, which show that change is taking place. Sometimes it may be helpful to identify these crucial indicators by using ranking exercises.

There is some debate about the extent to which indicators should be objectively verifiable; that is, that different people would take the same view about how change can be measured. At the initial planning stage, the different participants in a project should help to choose the indicators. Different groups of people are likely to choose different indicators according to what they think the project is trying to do, and the terms in which they see positive change. It is especially important to elicit the views of both women and men. It may be difficult to reach agreement on how change should be measured, but unless everyone involved is clear about what the project is trying to achieve, and the changes which should result, it is unlikely that the project will operate without conflicts which could damage its effectiveness. Discussion about the choice of indicators can reveal the different expectations among participants, and negotiations should continue until a satisfactory conclusion is reached.

As well as choosing indicators, decisions need to be made at the planning stage about how the information about them will be collected. This could be through regular reports and the keeping of registers, as part of the routine administration procedures; by research studies; or by special workshops. Indicators should be 'tracked' during implementation, as part of systematic monitoring, and it is likely that some may prove to be inappropriate and can be dropped. In some situations, tracking indicators can identify the distributional effects of a project, for example, the different effects of a forest protection project on people who are totally dependent on forest products compared to those who have other sources of livelihood.

In the case of project proposals whose objectives are initially very vague, such as 'to improve the quality of life' or 'to help people understand the forces that affect their lives', the process of deciding on indicators can be very helpful. By defining the actual changes which would need to take place in order for these objectives to be achieved, the objectives themselves can be made more realistic. 'Improving the quality of life' could be made more precise by identifying the indicators which would show the detailed improvements that are expected.

If programme objectives and indicators were not defined at the outset of a project then it will be necessary to define them when carrying out an evaluation. This can be done by asking the various parties involved to identify what they are actually doing, and what results they are expecting.

5.6 Who will manage the evaluation and who will carry it out?

Deciding who should be involved in any evaluation and on what terms, can be a cause of conflict. The decision should be negotiated in principle during the appraisal and planning stages of the project. The people who might be involved are:

- the men and women beneficiaries/users of the project

- project staff

- project management

- representatives of funding agencies: eg foreign NGO, UN, EEC, bilateral and multilateral agencies, local corporate donors

- local or national government officials

- consultants.

The different responsibilities, depending on the type and size of the project and the proposed evaluation, are:

- deciding that evaluation will happen

- funding the evaluation

- managing the evaluation

- carrying out the evaluation

- providing information.

Responsibility for ensuring that an evaluation is carried out will largely be determined by who is controlling it. This may be the implementing agency, project staff, the funders, the men and women at the grassroots, or a combination of these.

5.6.1 What skills are needed within the evaluation team?

Skills needed may be some or all of the following:

- ability to write a clear, concise report in language X
- ability to lead and manage an evaluation
- facilitation skills and knowledge of group dynamics
- capacity to analyse
- insight into the local situation, practices, beliefs
- knowledge of the country and the locality
- knowledge and experience of a particular type of work
- experience of participatory methods
- ease of access to women and men in the project area
- wide knowledge of the NGO scene in the country
- sound understanding of how interventions can affect men and women differently.

In an evaluation team, it is better to have members with different skills rather than expect to find one evaluator with every skill needed. Teams should be in proportion to the size of the work to be evaluated. Two to four may be a reasonable number, allowing different evaluators to look at different aspects of work. If there are evaluators who need translators this will also affect the team size. Obviously if the project or evaluation is very small then it is likely that one evaluator will be sufficient.

In some areas, projects and organisations have engaged in 'inter-project' evaluation, when staff of different organisations, undertaking fairly similar work, have evaluated each other. This is only effective where staff can trust each other.

5.6.2   Who can do the evaluation?

The choice of who should evaluate, will depend to a large extent on the purpose of the evaluation and the stage of the project at which the evaluation happens. (See Appendix 5 for the pros and cons of external and internal evaluation.)

Many women and men involved in a variety of development projects are actively involved in monitoring and evaluating their work (self-evaluation). But sometimes community members and project staff collect information to be analysed by other people, and never see the results. If they do eventually receive a report it may be in a language that they have difficulty understanding. If this happens evaluation can be seen negatively as something that is done by and for 'somebody else'.

The people who actually carry out the evaluation may be external evaluators, who are not part of the project, or staff members who have training or experience in evaluation, or a combination of these.

i. External evaluation
Traditional evaluation relies on formal short-term exercises done by outside 'experts', often reporting directly to the funding agency. The assumption is that people with no relationship to the project or organisation will make a more 'objective' assessment.

Formal external evaluation is appropriate when looking at issues of accountability, or if there is a need for particular expertise or experience which an external person might have. Such evaluations can be expensive, particularly when contracting international consultants who may cost many times more than locally contracted consultants in some places.

ii. Internal evaluation
Project staff with suitable training can carry out an evaluation, or a special evaluation function can be given to a group of staff. (A person from another part of the same organisation, but not directly involved in the project, may still be considered internal.)

Internal evaluation can contribute to increased understanding and better planning within a project, and help to strengthen the organisation, because reflection and learning is done by those people responsible for carrying out the work.

iii. Self-evaluation

A group of people can evaluate and make judgements and suggestions about work they are directly responsible for. Internal self-evaluation is valuable if done regularly as part of the normal project work, perhaps six-monthly or annually.

An outsider can be asked to help with the process. The outsider in this case is not an evaluator passing judgement, but someone who can help the group itself in its questioning.

iv. Joint evaluation

An evaluation can be undertaken jointly by different stakeholders. For example, the directors of a funding agency and the head of an implementing organisation may decide to carry out an evaluation. They would agree the terms of reference (see below) together and the evaluation could be carried out by one or more people chosen by them, either members of the organisations or external consultants. However, there is a danger that the evaluation team may become too large to function efficiently, because all the different stakeholders involved want to appoint someone to the team who will represent their views.

Many funders have tried to do this kind of evaluation in the spirit of partnership. But if the evaluation is insensitively imposed, and is closely related to questions of renewed funding, it is not truly a partnership.

5.6.3 Participatory evaluation

Participatory (or sometimes participative) evaluation involves the women and men staff and beneficiaries of a project. It can be an internal or external evaluation. True participation is when those involved are deciding and have control of the evaluation. They decide when it should happen, how it should be carried out, and by whom.

In its ideal form participatory evaluation is a way of doing evaluation which makes it an integral part of the planning and implementation of development action. The women and men directly involved in the project are at the centre of the process of evaluation. As a group, they come together to think about the project and what it has achieved.

Participatory evaluation is based on a people-centred approach to development and the belief that ordinary men and women have the capacity to change things. It is a form of learning, where the experience of the process of evaluation is as important as the findings. It is part of a whole approach to development, rather than a tool or technique that can be applied (as an afterthought) in any context. Project staff in a conventional top-down organisation cannot suddenly be expected to be confident participants in an evaluation; nor can they necessarily be expected to enable the confident participation of beneficiaries, when this has not previously been part of their way of working.

As with all evaluation, it is important to define clearly who is participating and on what terms. People often ask how they can make an evaluation 'as participative as possible', and if there are 'participatory techniques' they can use. But such questions show a lack of understanding about what participation really means, and its full implications.

Sometimes what is called participatory evaluation should more correctly be termed consultation. Different groups of men and women are asked their views about a project, or a community hosts the team of evaluators as they go about their field work. There is currently a growing interest in using so-called 'Participatory Rural Appraisal' techniques in an evaluation; but simply using the techniques will not in itself achieve real participation. Without real input and control in the design and implementation of the evaluation, people cannot be said to be truly participating.

However, there are occasions when a participatory approach is probably not appropriate; for example, when an audit is being carried out, or if there are serious management problems to be investigated.

5.6.4 User evaluation

This is a process in which the male and female beneficiaries or their representatives assess an organisation and/or the work it is promoting. These evaluations can be organised by the project participants themselves or by project staff, or by an external consultant.

It is important to ensure that the questions discussed are relevant to the participants, and the organisers should be honest about how much change is possible. Many apparently 'open' evaluations of this type have ended in demoralisation for the people taking part because of the limits to change.

Feeding back findings is important in all evaluation, but especially in this kind of exercise, where participants are being asked their views. It is important for project participants to know the reaction of project organisers to the findings. Such evaluations are a way of increasing accountability of funders and implementers to project beneficiaries, and require confidence on the part of project managers and staff.

5.7 How will the evaluation be done?

Answering questions about why and for whom an evaluation is being done, and who should do it, should make it easier to decide the approach that is appropriate and what methods and tools should be used. You will need to make choices about:

i. Formal or informal methods?
Formal methods:

• are carefully planned evaluation exercises, which have formal terms of reference(TOR)

• are special events at a particular stage of a project (eg, mid-term, final, ex-post)

• use external evaluators for increased accountability (this is often demanded by funders or government departments)

• cost more than informal exercises because of the need to contract consultants, the detailed preparation and the scope

• need a final comprehensive report

• can be disruptive to the rhythm of the project.

Informal methods:

• are simpler and do not require as much preparation as formal methods

• tend to be undertaken by people from the project itself or those associated with it

• may occur as regular events throughout the project, or as one-off events as and when needed

• are most appropriate for providing information for making decisions about the way a project is being implemented

• may need a short report documenting discussions, conclusions and recommendations, often only useful to those who participated. (Final project reports prepared by project staff, or half yearly internal evaluation meetings would fall into this category.)

ii. External or internal evaluators?
In the discussion on 'who' should be doing the evaluation (section 5.6), we looked at the relative pros and cons of internal and external exercises, as well as issues around participation. (See also Appendix 5.)

5.7.1 What information will be needed?

At the planning stage of a project, and certainly when discussing a proposal for support, it is important to build in the gathering of information, for on-going monitoring and later evaluation.

   Information needs are shaped by the purpose, scope and focus of an evaluation. They should relate to available resources, time frame, research and evaluation capacity at different levels.

i. Baseline information
The initial project document should provide information on a particular situation, location, the men and women who are the focus of a project, implementing agency and so on. Baseline information provides a point from which to measure change, to enable 'before' and 'after' comparisons to be made. Participatory appraisal studies are being increasingly used to provide this type of information.

If this is not possible an evaluation may compare the target group with similar groups of men and women who have not been involved in the project; but because of all the other factors affecting people's lives, it is difficult to identify causal links between the project and any differences which may be found.

ii. On-going information gathering

Workplans which state as clearly and simply as possible the objectives and what is expected of different project activities help to focus information gathering. At the planning stage of a project an evaluation plan can be worked out, which defines points in the life of projects (say quarterly, six-monthly or yearly) when results of activities and progress towards goals will be assessed. The plan should state how information on progress is to be gathered and by whom, what indicators will be used, and how the results will be fed back into on-going work.

It is helpful if yearly work plans fit into a system of longer-term goals. In this way progress can be reviewed annually, and overall direction modified as needed. Doing this can help projects bring work down to a more realistic level.

It is quite acceptable for project objectives and strategies to change as a result of on-going monitoring and evaluation. Any changes need to be agreed between the people concerned, recorded, and the reasons given. In terms of learning from development, it is as important to understand the processes at work, as to reflect on results.

iii. Existing information

Some of the evaluation questions may be answered by existing information. This could be:

• documents such as the diaries and notes of project workers, field visit reports, team meetings, and reports of evaluations that have been conducted at other times

• administrative documents of project staff

• information collected by other bodies that could provide background and comparative data eg official reports and research from government, UN and independent research institutes

- reports from other similar projects, especially data disaggregated by gender, area, age, or ethnic group.

iv. New information

It is important for issues of cost, time, practicality and usefulness to try and define *how* new information will be used, *when* it is needed and *the level of accuracy* required. The value of the information must match the resources needed for gathering it.

There are two main ways of collecting new information:

- questioning people through interviews, focus groups and conducting surveys

- observing people and things on site visits.

These techniques are often combined, for example the growing practice of rapid appraisal/assessment (RRA/PRA); knowledge, attitude and practice surveys (KAP); and case studies.

v. Quantitative or qualitative measures?

A good evaluation will use both quantitative and qualitative information. (See also the earlier discussions on measuring quantity and quality in section 4.3, and section 5.5.5 on the choice of indicators.) Quantitative information is often described as 'objective', yet someone has made a subjective judgement about what measure should be used as the standard! The relation between the two types of information is that quantitative data can be used for measuring 'what happened' (the changes which took place), and qualitative information can be used for analysing 'how and why' things happened.

Qualitative methods include observing activity, interviewing, and trying to gain a more complete understanding of complex changes. A criticism of qualitative data is that it is not 'representative', or scientific, and therefore generalisations cannot be drawn from it.

Studies are being done to compare information generated through these two methods, to see what the difference is in findings, versus relative costs.

5.8 How much will the evaluation cost, and what resources are needed?

At the planning stage of any project a budget should be drawn up to provide the resources needed for both monitoring and evaluation.

5.8.1 Budgeting for evaluation

When drawing up a budget, try to estimate all the expenses which might be incurred:

i. Financial costs
These will depend on the nature and size of the project or programme and the type of monitoring and evaluation envisaged. They will include:

- salaries of any people engaged for specific exercises

- daily expenses, travel costs (hire of vehicle, petrol)

- costs of meetings and workshops

- materials for production of reports and other methods of feedback.

If an organisation is planning an internal evaluation, the costs of this should be put into the budget. Costs might include the salary and expenses of a consultant to come and work with the team.

ii. Non-financial costs
There will be opportunity costs for project staff and participants, and others who may be asked to collaborate. People may be asked to spend time talking to external evaluators, or attending workshops, which will mean that other work will have to be rescheduled.

5.8.2 Matching scope to resources

The amount of money available will affect the scope and methods of evaluation. Some more formal quantitative techniques, such as full-scale surveys, can be more expensive than some of the less formal qualitative techniques carried out by project holders and participants themselves.

Evaluations with a greater degree of participation of the people concerned are likely to cost more in terms of time, and therefore of opportunity costs, at different stages of the evaluation process.

Clarity of purpose will help in deciding what resources should be used. For example, if evaluation is to provide information for internal decision making a less detailed exercise will probably be adequate. If the evaluation is to improve accountability, then the results should be detailed enough to provide this, and the cost of the evaluation will be correspondingly greater.

When drawing up a budget for a project, it can be helpful to have an agreed sum allowed for evaluation. Some of the official aid agencies allocate 5 per cent of programme budget for evaluation activity. For small projects, evaluation can be a relatively high percentage of overall costs.

5.9 Reporting back and follow up: how to make sure evaluation information is used

Deciding at the planning stage who needs to be told about the findings of the evaluation, and in what form, makes it more likely that an evaluation will be useful and have a positive effect. Different stakeholders will need different sorts of information, in different forms, for different uses.

5.9.1 The uses of evaluation results

Results can be used to:

• Improve organisation and management, particularly through enhanced communication between different levels of staff as a result of the evaluation exercise.

• Help in decision making, by indicating where action should be taken, where training or specialist help is needed, or where further research would be useful.

• Improve planning, by providing information about past performance, and influence policy making.

• Provide information for fundraising and advocacy, by demonstrating how needs can be met as a result of development activities, or by showing how some major constraints on development require action at national or international level.

• Improve public accountability, by demonstrating that resources have been used effectively.

5.9.2 How will findings be presented?

The product of internal and more informal exercises that are part of the ongoing routine of a project team may simply be a record of key discussion points and actions agreed, why and by whom.

More formal evaluation studies should produce a report. The format and style of the report should be made clear to whoever is responsible for writing it. (See terms of reference, section 6.3.2..) It may be necessary to present the report, or the summary, in a different form to the beneficiaries, perhaps by pictures or video to non-literate groups.

Resources may be needed for feedback workshops, seminars, preparation of reports and popular booklets, translated if necessary, as part of a strategy for sharing the findings of the evaluation with others working in similar fields.

5.9.3 Follow up

The evaluation should not be expected to come up with clear-cut, ready-made solutions. Evaluation can only provide the material for decision making, the decisions have to be made by those managing the project.

All those involved in the project should meet to discuss the issues raised by the evaluation and report, and decide about the follow-up measures, including a time frame for implementation. It may or may not be appropriate for staff of the funding NGO to attend such a meeting, or act as a facilitator, depending on what has been their role in the evaluation.

Beyond the level of the project, the results can be used to build up a picture of what does and does not seem to work in particular areas of work. This can feed into debates on policy and overall programme planning. It is also important to identify if there is information that could be valuable for larger debates on public policy, with major official funding agencies or government.

5.9.4 *Who owns evaluation and evaluation results?*

This relates to who is in charge of the evaluation process, and the way in which different people take part. If an outside agency carries out an external evaluation with little or no dialogue or negotiation with the project in question, it is likely that the project participants will not 'own' the process or findings. (They may also feel resentment at being used for someone else's research.) This is especially likely if there is no feedback of data to them. If the evaluation is intended to be truly participative, then a commitment to collective and individual ownership of the process and its outcomes is vital.

Where there are several major parties involved, conflict can arise where there has been insufficient clarity as to the purpose of the exercise. This may cause confusion regarding the relative emphasis to be given to the process of the evaluation compared to the product. For example, where one objective that has been identified is 'learning', then everyone also needs to be clear who is to do the learning, and in what way. Is the intention for the participants to learn from the experience of being involved in the process of evaluation, or are the funders anxious to learn, from a detailed report, whether their money is being wisely used? Or is the evaluation designed to enable both kinds of learning to take place? The team leader needs to be capable of interpreting the learning for the different parties.

There are ethical questions to be considered in relation to the use of information generated through evaluation. If a consultant is contracted to do an evaluation, or facilitate an internal exercise, clear rules must be established about what they can and cannot do with information gathered during the exercise. People giving information also need to feel sure that it will not be used against them, by getting into the wrong hands. Trust is an important ingredient in all evaluation work.

6 Some practical considerations when planning an evaluation

The previous section worked through the main questions that need to be dealt with when planning for monitoring and evaluation in the early stages of a project. This section will look in more detail at what is involved in carrying out a specific evaluation exercise. The process described is that of a formal exercise, but the method can be adapted to develop a plan of work for any type of evaluation or study.

6.1 Stages in evaluation

Whatever the purpose of an evaluation, or the methodology chosen, there are a number of distinct stages in the process:

1 Planning: deciding the purpose/s, questions and methods for the evaluation.

2 Managing: negotiating with others to plan the evaluation, prepare the terms of reference (TOR), select and supervise the evaluators, and decide how the results will be used.

3 Carrying out the evaluation: collecting and analysing the data, making conclusions and recommendations, writing a report in some form, and communicating the results.

4 Using the results: implementing recommendations, feeding into future planning, and sharing the lessons learnt.

Each of these activities may be carried out by a different person or group of people; for example, staff working for a funding NGO could be involved in any (or all) of these stages.

6.2 How to make sure an evaluation will be successful

Here are some reminders of points that have been made earlier:

• Be realistic about evaluation, recognise that it is a political process in which different views of development, hidden agendas, and unequal power relationships operate.

• Be clear about the purpose of a particular exercise and the key stakeholders involved.

• Negotiate priorities, and be clear about objectives; a single exercise cannot answer every question.

• Be clear about what evaluation can and cannot do. Do not use it for the wrong purposes. Evaluation is not the same as decision making.

• Plan evaluation activity as an integral part of project work, so that projects and programmes are designed with evaluation in mind. Discussing and planning for evaluation at an early stage ensures that people expect it to happen, and so feel less threatened by it when it does happen.

• Be clear about what people's responsibilities are in different evaluation exercises, so that they know what is expected of them.

• Choose an approach and methods appropriate to the type of work being evaluated and the questions being asked.

• Involve people, particularly those who will use the information, from the outset, so they 'own' the process, and will make use of the findings.

• Be prepared to adapt and refine plans so that evaluation can be carried out at an appropriate time.

• Encourage feelings of respect and trust among all involved.

6.3 Planning and managing an evaluation

Detailed planning should start well in advance. Check that the plans for evaluation made at the assessment stage of the project are still valid; it may be that the passage of time and the development of the project, or the quality of monitoring, makes the original plans redundant.

A meeting of the stakeholders should be called by the person organising the evaluation, to confirm the underlying principles of the original plan, and establish the operational details. If the evaluation is to be on a large scale, you may need to appoint a 'steering committee'. Make sure that everybody feels confident that their interests will be faithfully represented by this committee.

The stakeholders need to reach agreement on the principal objectives of the evaluation. There are likely to be some obvious objectives, which everyone will agree about, but other objectives may be put forward which are only regarded as important by an individual. It is not always possible to reach consensus, and the power relations between the stakeholders may be such that one party may have more authority. For example, a major funder may insist on external evaluation when there is a question of further funding. Usually, however, there is a lot of scope for discussion about specific evaluation objectives, and the methods to be used; and some bilateral and multilateral funders are very open to suggestions from funding NGOs about methodology.

It may not be possible to dispel entirely the fears of some participants about a planned evaluation. The value of their efforts is to come under scrutiny, and they may themselves have a very high personal investment in the work. For this reason, any evaluation that may affect funding decisions should happen well before the end of the funding period, and a sufficient winding-down period should be allowed (this may be a year or more).

In order to make sure that the evaluation is useful, it is vital to consult the people who are most likely to be able to use the results, at an early stage. This can avoid a waste of time and effort in collecting information which is unnecessary. If people are asked beforehand about the kind of information which they would find relevant, they are much more likely to find the results of the evaluation of interest to them, and to make use of the findings when planning for the future.

Agreeing on priorities can help to limit the scope of the

evaluation, and make it more manageable. If necessary, ranking methods can be used to help people reach agreement about the purposes and the questions to be asked. Once everyone involved is clear about the main purposes of the evaluation, then it is easier to settle questions of method and approach. It is always easier to negotiate when the various parties are open about what they really want. For example, if the evaluation is intended to increase accountability, and, in addition, a major funder is planning to use the results of the evaluation in coming to a decision on extending the funding, then this latter consideration should be freely acknowledged, so that there are no false expectations.

You should allow plenty of time for the planning of a major evaluation, to make sure everyone involved, or at least everyone on the steering committee, is able to take part in meetings and decide on a final plan.

6.3.1 Drawing up the terms of reference (TOR)

Many evaluations suffer from the over-wide scope of the exercise. The terms of reference (TOR) become a shopping list, rather than a guide to focus the work.

The TOR set out the formal agreements about the evaluation, its scope, purpose, and the methods to be used, and outline the specific tasks of the evaluation team leader. Those managing the evaluation process are responsible for drawing up the TOR. Where more than one person or agency is involved, it should be agreed who has ultimate authority. It may take several attempts before the final version of the TOR is agreed by everyone. It is important that the TOR incorporate a gender perspective.

Good TOR pave the way for a good evaluation, acting as a point of reference throughout. They should be drawn up well in advance of the date of the evaluation, in order to allow adequate time for planning, selecting and employing evaluators, sorting out the logistics, and briefing everyone involved. The TOR should reflect both the needs of staff and others involved to learn from their experience, and the need of the organisations to improve performance and accountability. Evaluators may help to draw up the TOR and should be asked to review and comment on them before beginning the evaluation. A good evaluator is likely to raise questions about the initial TOR.

6.3.2 Contents of the TOR

Terms of reference should cover:

1 **Background:** purpose and objectives of activity, work, project or programme to be evaluated.

2 **Objectives:** major issues to be addressed, what the evaluation is expected to find out, the questions to be answered.

3 **Methods:** visits, review of documentary material, data-collection, interviews, workshops.

4 **Timetable:** schedule for the major activities (e.g. pre-visits, field work, writing, feedback) of the evaluation and its completion date.

5 **Products:** the products required from the evaluation exercise, (e.g. report, workshop), who is responsible for producing them, who will present them, who the reports are for. The length, format and language of the main report and executive summary should be indicated. The team leader is usually the person responsible for the completion of the formal report. The process of follow-up should be noted.

6 **The evaluation team:** the person specifications (mandatory and desired) of each team member, the number of team members, the ideal combination of skills and experience at team level (including language requirements, gender balance, and understanding of gender issues).

7 **Budget and logistics:** details of the main expenses (e.g. salaries, expenses, travel, lodging, communications). Financial reporting requirements (e.g. reimbursement for actual, or per diems). Logistical support being offered (e.g. vehicles, office space, computer facilities, secretarial help), and how, where and by whom this will be made available.

8 **Use of information:** extent of confidentiality, ownership of the report.

9 **Terms of reference for evaluation leader:** the team leader of the evaluation must be given an individual TOR outlining his/her specific tasks and responsibilities, particularly any writing and managerial tasks.

6.3.3 Confidentiality

The TOR should state any conditions about the subsequent use of information gained during the exercise, by all team members. This should cover both general confidentiality and the ownership of the specific report. The evaluation team has access to a great amount of confidential information about the funding agency, the implementing NGO, and their personnel, men and women at the grassroots. It is crucial that the terms on which this information is provided are made clear to all concerned at the outset. Similarly, the evaluators need to have confidence that they can be candid in their observations and recommendations, without fear that these will be circulated indiscreetly.

6.3.4 Recruitment and selection of evaluators

Choosing evaluators with the appropriate skills and experience is important to the success of an evaluation. The purpose, the methods chosen, the type and size of the project or programme, and the budget available will determine whom to recruit. You should consider the following points:

1 The range of skills and experience needed. This includes the issue of communication between the evaluator and the subject of evaluation e.g. if the evaluator cannot speak the language, good interpreters will also have to be hired, or if it is not acceptable for men to speak with women in a particular society, it will be necessary to have a women with the relevant skills on the team.

2 The gender balance, and gender-awareness, of the team.

3 The balance between evaluation skills, technical knowledge, and in-depth local knowledge. Remember that, while empathy and knowledge are important, bringing in people with a different cultural perspective can be stimulating; for example, people with

experience of working within governments, as well as those from an NGO background.

At least two to three months may be needed to recruit suitable evaluators. Good consultants are likely to be booked up for several months in advance. Use the widest possible network of contacts to identify candidates. Sources include other donors, academic institutions (local and international), partner organisations. Experience is very important. Evaluators should have experience of similar evaluations, and an understanding of the kind of work or project involved, and at least some members of the team should have a good knowledge of the country, and of the local situation.

Once references have been checked and consultants selected, the TOR should be discussed with evaluators before a contract is agreed. Staff of funding NGOs must be sure to observe the terms of the recruitment policies of their organisation. Contracts for individual members of the team should specify the written reports that they will be expected to prepare; clarity about this aspect of the work will be helpful to the team leader.

6.3.5 Essential documentation

Evaluators need to see all the relevant internal and external or background documentation (annual reports, copies of previous evaluations, project and programme documentation, including financial details, and policy statements). Collating and analysing this data may help to identify some questions the evaluation should try to answer. It is important that the evaluators understand fully the basic assumptions behind the decision to support or set up the work under review; and whether the initial objectives have been changed significantly.

6.3.6 Orientation and briefing

Whoever is responsible for the overall management of the evaluation must arrange orientation and briefing for the evaluators. Background material should be sent to them beforehand. The aim of orientation is to give a management and administrative brief on the exercise, answer any queries, and review the workplan. The evaluators must be told to whom they are to report. They should also be told about accountancy procedures for expenses.

The evaluators might also need to meet other people involved, as part of their orientation; for example, the people who are asking for the exercise, especially in order that the evaluators gain insight as to how the findings may be used; funders; policy makers; and managers.

The orientation period allows for team building between the evaluators before they start their field work, which can be particularly important where team members have not worked together before, and come from different backgrounds. It should also be used for the preparation of a more detailed workplan, as well as deciding details of data collection methods, and practical logistics. It is often impossible for evaluators to interview all those involved or affected by a project, or visit every project site. A representative sample has to be chosen. Evaluators should explain in their report why they chose the particular sites to visit and persons to interview.

Plenty of time should be allowed for the orientation period. The manager of the evaluation should check again, before the evaluation starts, that all those involved are clear about the overall purpose of the evaluation, the way it is to be done, and individual roles and responsibilities.

6.3.7 Resources and logistical arrangements

Evaluators need somewhere quiet to work together and write up their reports, where they will not be interrupted. Any group meetings should take place in surroundings which encourage concentration and reflection. The evaluation team should stay together, in the same accommodation, which should be suitably furnished and equipped (for example, with tables to write at, computing facilities, flip chart paper, and so on).

It may be useful to appoint a link person to deal with detailed logistical arrangements, so that last-minute changes can be handled with the minimum of disruption. The arrangements for the use and maintenance of vehicles should be clear.

6.4 Field work

The purpose of field work is to collect information which would not otherwise be available. It also allows the evaluation team to gain their own perspective from which to judge the work. Any new information generated through an evaluation should be integrated into the body of information available within the project itself. Field work usually consists of a mixture of some of the following:

• structured surveys

• interviews/conversations with individuals and groups affected by the project, both inside and outside the specific target groups

• interviews with key people outside the project

• visits to other projects addressing similar problems

• organised seminars and /or interviews with target groups, project staff, partners and other relevant people

• group discussions

• observations.

6.5 Management and supervision of the exercise

The evaluation manager is responsible for ensuring that the exercise keeps on course and to schedule. Regular communication should ensure that work is progressing as planned and any problems are dealt with as they arise, then any adjustments can be agreed and made before it is too late.

It is sometimes helpful for a pre-visit to be made to the project by a member of the evaluation team, probably the team leader, to clarify what each party hopes to gain from the exercise, and agree the final operational details. This is a chance for people to get to know one another, and for the evaluator to discuss preparatory tasks, so that data is ready for the main visits. The costs and benefits of such a visit need to be carefully considered. The advantage of setting up preparatory work, and of the initial human contact, should not be underestimated. Pre-visits can be used to clarify the exact purposes of an evaluation which a project has requested.

The relationship between the evaluation team and the people whose work is being evaluated can make or break the exercise. Issues have to be raised in a constructive way, helping the people concerned to confront assumptions. To be too critical may be counter-productive; to recognise efforts and discuss alternatives creatively is a better approach. Everyone must understand that the evaluation team is not going to provide a miracle solution: the remedies lie in the hands of the people who are going to have to see the work through after the evaluators have left.

Meetings should be arranged at convenient times, so that the evaluation team is seen to be accessible to all the women and men involved. It is also important that people who find it difficult to speak out in a large meeting are given some other opportunity to put forward their views.

6.6 Arranging meetings

Any evaluation will require at least three formal meetings between the evaluation team and representatives of the people whose work is being evaluated:

Initial meeting: this takes place before field work starts, to clarify the objectives of the exercise and to make sure that the views of the people responsible for the work are known.

Mid-way meeting: this takes place mid-way through the exercise to share initial findings and obtain feedback on preliminary analysis. Where possible, evaluators should circulate their findings in advance of the meeting so that feedback can be prepared.

Final meeting: this takes place at the end of the field work, with the evaluation team, to share preliminary conclusions and to obtain feedback on findings. Again, if appropriate, the evaluators should circulate their conclusions in advance of the meeting, so that project staff and others directly involved have time to meet among themselves and discuss them. Errors of fact can be corrected, and the evaluators can find out people's reactions.

6.7 Analysis

The evaluators have the task of analysing the information collected. They will be looking at processes, relationships and interactions in the project, and gaining an overview of what has happened.

Different evaluations will have different emphases, but in general the evaluators will try to give an account of the context of the project, and its capacity to deal with the problems it was set up to address, the factors which have contributed to the success of the project, the major constraints, and, overall, whether the project has been worth the effort.

The meetings with project staff during the course of the evaluation provide an opportunity to check that the developing analysis of the situation is correct.

6.8 Conclusions and recommendations

The conclusions reached by the evaluators should provide answers to the evaluation questions, and be based on the information collected. If it was difficult to get the necessary information, or if there are conflicting views within the evaluation team, this should be made clear.

As well as describing the main achievements and failures, the findings should point to any continuing constraints that can affect future work, particularly constraints beyond the control of the project organisers. The findings should not be simply a list of facts, but look critically at the effect of the project, and any obvious reasons for the situation.

Recommendations should be based on findings. They should be practical and feasible, and point out what needs to be done, build on achievements, solve problems and counter constraints. The time-scale should be made clear, and recommendations divided into short, medium, and long-term.

Recommendations should be prioritised, and directed to particular people or groups. Keeping in mind, throughout the exercise, the person or group for whom the recommendations are intended, can help the evaluator to produce sharply-focused and relevant suggestions. It can be useful to list recommendations for the project to address, and those for the funder to address.

6.9 Writing the final report

As far as possible, writing up and preliminary reporting on the evaluation should be done before the evaluation team leaves the area. This is very important where a team of evaluators are working together, because it is often difficult for them to meet again afterwards because of other commitments and the fact that they may live in different parts of the world. Contracts with consultants should stipulate that full payment will only be made when a satisfactory final report has been submitted. It should be made clear how reports are to be presented, and that an executive summary, at the beginning of the final report, is essential.

6.9.1 The contents of the report

The report should be written with the main users in mind: who needs what information in what form? Project managers will find detailed, technical information helpful. Other people less directly involved, but interested, need a short summary.

There is no set rule about the length of a report, but it should not be so long that nobody will read it! Supporting information should be in the form of accompanying documents, or appendices, rather than overloading the main report. Evaluators should consider whether the work that goes into writing will be in proportion to the expected usefulness of the report and the overall scope of the evaluation. Appendix 4 suggests a plan for the contents of a report.

The summary should provide sufficient information about the main conclusions and recommendations reached in the report for managers to be able to get a quick grasp of the important issues. The rest of the material will be used primarily by these working at the various levels of the project, to help with further planning and implementation.

The analysis and line of argument used in reaching various conclusions, as well as the information on which they are based, should be clearly stated, to encourage discussion on the possible actions to be taken. If lists of recommendations are given without explanations, and the reasons behind them are not easy to see, then their relevance to the project will be lost.

7 Using evaluation: feedback and follow-up

This section covers the initial feedback on the evaluation report through to the broader question of how the experience can shape future practice.

7.1 Initial feedback

The report should be made available both to those responsible for, and those affected by, the work which has been the subject of the evaluation. This is the moment to correct errors of fact, or interpretation.

The report will then be formally submitted for circulation and internal discussion before a further meeting with the evaluation team. For example, if the evaluation has been commissioned by a local NGO, then the NGO will be responsible for collating views on the report and gathering responses to the conclusions and recommendations. Usually, it will want to forward a copy of the main findings to its funder, especially if there are implications which will need to be discussed with them. If the evaluation has been commissioned by a funding agency, then it will determine the process by which the findings are fed back. A funder should make clear what, if any, implications it sees for the future relationship with the group whose work it funds.

If the report does not fully answer the TOR, then the person managing the evaluation should indicate this to the evaluation team leader. A decision will need to be made about what action needs to be taken. In extreme cases payment may be withheld until a satisfactory report is received.

7.2 Follow-up

Once the findings have been assimilated, a follow-up meeting should be called to resolve any points of clarification and to come to agreement about what actions need to be taken. This must be sensitively handled. It may be that the findings of the evaluation reveal unintended harmful effects of the work which was evaluated, for example, that the river is being polluted; women are worse off than they were before; or children's nutritional status is deteriorating.

The evaluation process itself may have uncovered problems in the relationship between the funding agency and the group whose work is being funded, which will have to be addressed.

In extreme cases, the agency may decide to stop funding on the basis of the findings — or the local group may decide to cease or radically re-direct its work. It may be that the findings reveal serious differences between the criteria of the funding agency and those of the group it has been supporting.

Where it is agreed by all concerned that changes are required, the funding agency may help by paying for someone to work alongside the local group to help them to consider the detailed implications of the evaluation and re-plan accordingly.

The funding agency will either have to agree with the proposed course of action to implement or act on the evaluation findings; or, if it is apparent that the time has come to end the funding, then a programme for how this will happen over time should be mapped out.

7.3 Dissemination

Whatever the outcome, a decision should be made as to what aspects of the findings of the evaluation should be disseminated further, how and to whom. Issues of confidentiality will need to be borne in mind. Those who have furnished information for an evaluation have a right to be told of the outcome.

Formal reports are normally circulated in their entirety to the local NGO, the funders and those who commissioned the study (if different). The executive summary accompanying the formal report can be circulated more widely as a stand-alone document to those engaged in similar work, relevant official bodies, and NGO staff involved in policy development.

Other forms of dissemination might be:

• a workshop of people interested in similar areas of work, to discuss the findings;

• production of a booklet or other materials for dissemination at grassroots level;

• a case study of the experience for publication.

7.4 Institutional learning

One of the purposes of an evaluation is to enable as many people as possible, within and outside the organisation concerned, to learn from what has been done with a view to improving future practice. Significant policy and practical issues which have emerged from the exercise, in terms of the work evaluated, methods of evaluation, and the agency's own policy and practice, should be highlighted, recorded, disseminated, and discussed.

A systematic review of the evaluation exercise itself should also form part of the final learning process and should cover:

• objectives of the evaluation exercise

• logistics

• methods used and approach

• implementation of the evaluation plan

• whether the findings justified the expense (time and money).

This would usually be a confidential, internal document.

7.5 Barriers to learning and change

Will the lessons learned as a result of an evaluation be incorporated into future practice, either at the level of a specific project, or in the organisations involved? The resources used on an exercise will have been wasted if nothing happens, and the same mistakes are repeated in future.

There are various factors that affect whether learning is likely to happen within a project or organisation. For example, the climate for change: are people open to critical reflection? The importance of 'ownership' of the evaluation and findings has already been stressed. Other factors relate to 'bureaucratic inertia', to personal 'territory' and jobs, and simple expediency. People may be very reluctant to face changes to the way they have been doing things, and may see any proposed change as a threat to their status or security.

A funding agency has a responsibility to make the best possible use of the resources entrusted to it. If resources of money, time, and energy have been spent on an evaluation, then it is the responsibility of everyone concerned to make the fullest possible use of the findings, to improve future practice.

Appendix 1 Checklist of questions

If you are contemplating evaluation, it may help to clarify your thinking if you work through this list of questions.

Is it an evaluation you want?

1 Why?

Why do you want to do an evaluation?
Why is an evaluation being called for?
Is it really an evaluation that needs to be done? Maybe some other exercise would be more appropriate: management review; problem-solving exercise; financial audit; skills training; research-assessment of needs.

2 For whom?

Who is asking for the exercise?
Who are the key parties who have an interest in the exercise?
Are they one and the same?

3 What?

What is it that is to be evaluated?
What are the key questions — and who is interested in these?
Is it a realistic task?

4 How will it be done?

As a participatory exercise, perhaps with an external 'facilitator'?
As an external quantitative evaluation?

As an external evaluation focusing on qualitative aspects?
Or some combination of the above?

5 Who will do it?

Who will be in charge of the exercise, coordinate it, make sure it happens?
Who decides the process/form of the evaluation?
Who is going to do the actual evaluation: an outsider; a team from outside; some outsiders together with those involved in the work to be evaluated; or the team involved themselves?
Who chooses who is going to do the exercise?
Should you be advertising if you need external help? Where are you looking?
Are there people within the organisation who have the skills that you are looking for?
How will people taken on especially for the work be contracted or seconded? Who has to do this?
Have you considered the male/female balance in the team?
Have the evaluators got the expertise for the type of evaluation you want?

6 Terms of reference

Do you need to draw up terms of reference?
How will these be drawn up?
Who is responsible for drafting them?
How are you going to make sure that all key actors are enabled to feed in their concerns and ideas?
How will you ensure that gender considerations are clearly stated?
Who will have final say in terms of what can and can't be looked at?
To whom should the draft be circulated to for comments/ information?

7 Time

How long will it take?
Have you allowed enough time to cover the whole exercise; to

allow for a full planning process; pre-visits or studies that should be made, and preliminary research; the main research period; report writing; feedback, discussion and implementation of recommendations; workshops to disseminate findings more widely?

8 Information

What are the key questions (how have these been defined)?
What are the information sources?
How accessible are they?
What ground work needs to be done in preparation?
How will information be collected?
How will it be analysed?
How will findings be communicated and to whom?
Will there be a report? In what format? For whom? Who will compose it?
Will there be an initial circulation list already agreed to see and discuss the first draft?
Will there be other kinds of feedback? For/by whom? What form (workshop/seminar)?

9 How much will it cost?

When you are budgeting for the exercise have you taken full account of all the expenses to be incurred?
What resources are needed (human, financial, infrastructure, administrative)?
Who is going to finance the exercise, from what budget?

10 Planning and management

What needs to be done by whom, by when?

11 Constraints

Have you considered what the constraints might be and how you can minimise or overcome them (seasons, weather, public

holidays, political events, hidden agendas and sensitivities)?
Is what you want to evaluate in an 'evaluable' state?
Will you be constrained by lack of time or money?

12 Conflict

What procedures have been worked out to solve any question of conflict in relation to the Terms of Reference, method, outcome, follow-up?

13 Evaluation

How will you evaluate the evaluation exercise (design, process, implementation, follow-up, effort expended against results and costs)?

Appendix 2 Developing an evaluation plan

Managing an evaluation

(This section and the following one are based on material contained in Policy and Procedure Manual, Draft, April 1990, Appendix D, produced by UNICEF Evaluation Office, New York.)

1 Planning

Involve key stakeholders in discussion on evaluation purpose(s).
Decide on key evaluation questions.
Select main approach and methods based on key questions.
Prepare an overall plan.
Prepare TOR/ ensure necessary people involved in feeding into them.
Recruit evaluation team as appropriate.
Select participants in team.
Ensure key material is collected for background and briefing of team.
Ensure logistics are in place, and in particular that team will have reasonable conditions for meeting and writing.

2 Implementation

Ensure team have sufficient briefing, parameters of organisation, are clear what is being asked of them.
Ensure responsibility for final product is understood.
Ensure evaluation team know who key link people are.
Supervise exercise and provide on-going support as necessary.
Attend meeting for preliminary discussion of findings and recommendations.

Review draft report and give comments to team. Schedule debriefing session with team and sponsors (as appropriate). Promote evaluation of evaluation by different parties.

3 Follow up

Meet with project to discuss implementation. Discuss and agree wider distribution of report of evaluation, and any adaptations necessary. Promote wider dissemination of findings and learning. Encourage use of results in future programming (for example promote follow up meeting 6 and 12 months later to see what changes have been made following the exercise — why/why not).

Appendix 3 Tasks for the team leader

Preliminary questions: are you being asked to do something sensible? Is the task do-able, is the work evaluable? What are the different agendas? Is evaluation being used to fudge other actions which should be taken more directly? Is the organisation or group in question in crisis?

i. Planning

Review the TOR with the manager of the exercise — discuss and revise as necessary.

Ensure you are aware of evaluation 'sponsors' and key stakeholders. As far as possible appraise yourself of their agendas and key purposes in the exercise.

Refine evaluation design and methods as needed.

Meet/contract other team members.

Ensure people are clear and happy about contractual arrangements — ensure other members have sufficient experience to produce the work that will be required.

Ensure gender balance in team and gender expertise. Ensure logistics will enable accessing women's views and information as much as men, at minimum.

Ensure those promoting evaluation are preparing background documentation, request further information as appropriate.

Investigate possible pre visit to project/organisation to set up any necessary preparation work by team, or data collection. This may involve a training element.

Select sample sites as appropriate.

Ensure you will have sufficient time for team building in initial days of exercise, and sufficient time for evaluation team to meet during field work and concluding phases.

Ensure logistical back-up is available, and find out who is your link person.

Find out if translators are needed, and available, and of a reasonable standard.

ii. Implementation
Hold initial meetings at project site.
Collect data: project records, existing data, interviews, surveys, observation.
Analyse data.
Write first draft of evaluation report.
Give preliminary feed back to project holders/evaluation manager/sponsors
Review report on basis of comments (correct facts).
Produce final report, or any other products envisaged.

iii. Follow up
Debrief evaluation promoters, content of findings and evaluation of process.
Ensure compliance with any accounting procedures, and ensure payment has been authorised.

Appendix 4 Suggestions for content of an evaluation report

If you are contracting someone to do an evaluation, it is useful to give them clear guidance on the report that is required. Likewise, if you are evaluating, be clear what is being expected of you, and whether there are specific formats you will be required to follow. Keep reports short! Otherwise they risk being unread. Here is an outline of what a report should cover:

Title page: name of service, programme, or project evaluated; name and address of the organisation the report is submitted to; names and organisations of the evaluators; dates of evaluation; date of completion of report.

Contents list, with page numbers

Acknowledgements (if appropriate): thanks to those who helped or advised the evaluators.

Executive summary: summary of the activity evaluated, the purpose of the evaluation, the methods used, the major findings, most important recommendations, any general conclusions. This should be only two or three sides, and able to act as a 'stand-alone' document for people who will not receive the full report.

Introduction: full description of the activity being evaluated, giving the history, context, aims and objectives, beneficiaries, method of funding; summary of purposes of evaluation, who the evaluation was for, description of evaluation team, date of evaluation.

Evaluation: list of objectives of the evaluation, and the questions to be answered; full description of evaluation process: data collected, methods of data collection and analysis, sites visited, and reasons for choice of methods and visits; any constraints or problems in carrying out the evaluation.

Findings: clear statement of what the evaluation found out in response to the questions it was set up to answer; data collected, presented graphically where possible, in tables and figures; basis for judgements about the progress of the activity in respect of its original or modified objectives; reasons for identified successes and failures; any unexpected, but relevant, findings; continuing constraints on activity.

Recommendations: recommendations, linked to findings, listed in order of importance, with each recommendation directed at a specific person or group of people; costs of recommendations in terms of resources; list of decisions to be made, and the people who should make them; proposed timetable for implementation of recommendations.

General conclusions: lessons learned from this evaluation, for those planning, implementing or evaluating similar activities.

Appendices: list of people interviewed, sites visited; tools used for data collection (e.g. questionnaires); Terms of Reference; abbreviations, glossary; full details of costs of evaluation.

Appendix 5 Advantages and disadvantages of external and internal evaluators

Internal evaluator

Advantages

Knows the organisation, its programme, ethos, and ways of working.
Understands and can interpret personal behaviour and attitudes.
Because known to staff, less likely to cause anxiety or disruption.
Better able to follow up on recommendations.
Usually less expensive.
Doesn't require lengthy recruitment procedures.
Helps to develop internal evaluation capacity, at country or national level.
Better able to communicate evaluation findings throughout organisation.

Disadvantages

Finds it harder to be objective.
May avoid negative conclusions, which reflect badly on individuals or the organisation.
Tends to accept assumptions of organisation uncritically.
May be constrained by demands of existing job (if seconded to an evaluation) and not able to give sufficient time to evaluation.
May be part of authority structure, involved in internal politics or conflicts.
May not be fully trained or experienced in evaluation.
May not have necessary technical expertise.

External evaluator

Advantages

Not personally involved, so more objective.
Free from organisational bias, can contribute fresh perspective.
May have broader experience in field.
May be trained and experienced in carrying out evaluations.
Can act as arbitrator or neutral mediator in cases where evaluation reveals conflicts of interest.
May contribute technical knowledge or advice.

Disadvantages

May not fully understand the organisation policies, procedures, personalities and ethos.
May not appreciate local political and cultural environment.
May not appreciate constraints on implementing recommendations.
May be seen as critical adversary, arousing anxiety and defensiveness.
May be expensive.
Takes time to recruit, brief, and orientate.
Less likely to be able to follow-up on implementation of recommendations.

References and further reading

---

1 Books on evaluation on which this guide is based:

AGKED and MISEREOR *Evaluations in the Churches' Development Cooperation: A Workbook for Implementing Partner Organisations and Support Agencies*
AGKED, Kniebisstr. 29, D-7000 Stuttgart 1, or MISEREOR, Mozartstr. 9, D-5000 Aachen, June 1991, 90 pp.

Beaudoux, E. et al *Supporting Development Action at Community Level: A Methodological Guide*
Macmillan/COTA 1992 187pp.

Feuerstein, M-T *Partners in Evaluation: Evaluating Development and Community Programmes with Participants*
Macmillan, TALC, 1986, 196 pp.

(The same book is translated into Portuguese : *Avaliação: como avaliar programas de desenvolvimento com a participação da comunidade*, ISBN 85-05-01098-1 Edicoes Paulinas, Sáo Paulo, 1990. Available through ARTHAG.)

NORAD, *Guide to Planning and Evaluating NGO Projects*
Part 1 — Principles and Policies of Development Assistance pp.25.
Part 2 — Core Elements in Planning Development assistance pp.42
Part 3 — Project implementation pp.35
Norwegian Agency for Development Cooperation (NORAD), Division for Non-Governmental Organisations, Oslo, Norway.
English translated from Norwegian March 1989.

UNICEF, *Guide for Monitoring and Evaluation*
Evaluation office UNICEF, 3 UN Plaza, New York, NY 10017USA.
131pp. Also in French and Spanish. UNICEF publishes a wide
range of material on evaluation in a variety of languages.

Willot, P *'L'auto-evaluation Assistée'*, pp.27, 1982, Centre pour la
recherche interdisciplinaire sur le developpement (CRID) rue
Valduc, 152, B-1160 Brussels, Belgium.
(Only available in French.

Choudhary A and Tandon R *Pariticpatory Evaluation: Issues and
concerns*, PRIA, New Delhi, 80pp.

2 Further reading on evaluation and project planning:

Anderson M B and Woodrow P J *Rising from the Ashes: Development
Strategies in Times of Disaster*.
Westview Press/UNESCO, Paris, 1989.

Carr, M., de Crombrugghe, G. and Howes, M. *Assessing
Development Projects:An Approach to Evaluation as if People Mattered*
Le Collective d'Echanges pour la Technologie Approprie (COTA),
Rue de la Sabonniere 18, B-1000 Brussels, October 1984, pp.40 plus
appendices

Casley, D. J. and Kumar, K. *The Collection, Analysis, and Use of
Monitoring and Evaluation Data*
A World Bank Publication, John Hopkins Press, Baltimore, 1988,
180 pages

Coleman, G 'Project planning: logical framework approach to the
monitoring and evaluation of agricultural and rural development
projects', in *Project Appraisal* vol 2 no 4 1987 pp 251 — 259.

Eade D and Williams SW, *The Oxfam Handbook: Development and
Relief*. Oxfam, Oxford, 1995. (The Resources Directory gives
addresses of organisations who are likely to publish books on
evaluation in various languages.)

Forum Valutazione, periodical with a variety of articles on evaluation in Englaish, Spanish, Italian, French, produced by CISP, Via Marianna Dioigi, 57 00193 Roma

Herman, J L., Morris, L L. and Fitz-Gibbon, C. T. *Program Evaluator's Kit*
  1 Evaluator's handbook
  2 How to focus an evaluation
  3 How to design a program evaluation
  4 How to use qualitative methods in evaluation
  5 How to assess program implementation
  6 How to measure attitudes
  7 How to measure performance and use tests
  8 How to analyze data
  9 How to communicate evaluation findings

Hope A and Timmel S *Training for Transformation: A Handbook for Community Workers*. Mambo Press, Gweru, Zimbabwe 1987

Kabeer, N. 'Gender, development and training: raising awareness in the planning process', in *Development in Practice*, vol 1, no 3 1991, Oxfam

Marsden, D. and Oakley, P. (eds) *Evaluating Social Development Projects*, Oxfam Development Guidelines Series No. 5
Oxfam, Oxford, 1990, 162 pp

Moser, C O N 'Gender planning in the Third World: meeting practical and strategic gender needs', *World Development* vol 17, 11 1989

Moser, C O N *Gender Planning and Development Theory, Practice, and Training*
Routledge, London and New York, 1993 285pp

Narayan, D *Participatory Evaluation: Tools for Managing Change in Water and Sanitation, Technical Paper 207*.
World Bank, 1993.

Parker, A R, *Another Point of View: A Manual on Gender Analysis Training for Grassroots Workers.*
UNIFEM, 1993.

Patton, M. Q. *Qualitative Evaluation and Research Methods*
Sage Publications, 28 Banner Street, London EC14 8QE,1990
(2nd ed.), 500 pages

Patton, M. Q. *Utilization focused evaluation*
Sage Publications,1978.

Patton M Q *Practical Evaluation*
Sage Publications, 1982 319pp

Pfohl, J, *Participatory Evaluation: A User's Guide.*
USAID Sri Lanka, 1986. Available from PACT.

Programme for International Development, Clark University,
An Introductin to Participatory Rural Appraisal for Rural Resource Management.
Clark University, Worcester, Mass. and National Environment
Secretariat, Ministry of Environment and Natural Resources,
nairboi, Kenya, 1989.

Rao, A., Anderson, M B., Overholt C A. *Gender Analysis in Development Planning: A Casebook,* Kumarian Press, 1991

Reading Rural Development Communications, *'Bulletin 14'* —
March/April 1982, University of Reading Agricultural and
Rural Development Centre.
(Special issue on evaluation. Includes Oakley P 'Evaluating
social development: how much or how good?' and Feuerstein M
T 'Participatory evaluation: by, with and for the people'.)

Riddell, R. *Judging Success: Evaluating NGO Approaches to Alleviating Poverty in Developing Countries*
ODI, Working Paper 37, London, May 1990, 50 pages

Robinson M and Thin N *Project Evaluation: A Guide for NGOs*
ODA, 1993, 40pp.

Rugh, J. *Self-Evaluation: Ideas for Participatory Evaluation of Rural Community Development Projects*
World Neighbours Publication, Oklahoma City, 1986, 42 pp.

Sartorious, R F 'The logical framework approach to project design and management', in *Evaluation Practice* vol 12 no 2 1991 pp 139-147.

SCF Toolkits: Gosling L with Edwards M, *Assessment, Monitoring, Review and Evaluation.*
SCF, 1994.

Srinivasan, L *Tools for Community Participation: A Manual for Training Trainers in Participatory Techniques.*
PROWWESS/UNDP Technical Series, 1990.

Thomas-Slayter B and Esser A L, *Tools of Gender Analysis: A Guide to Field Methods for Bringing Gender ito Sustainable Resource Management.*
ECOGEN Research Project, Internal Development Programme, Clark University, Worcester, Mass., 1993.

Zivetz, Laurie *Project Identification, Design and Appraisal: A Manual for NGOs,* ACFOA, Canberra, 1990

3 Further reading on Rapid Rural Appraisal and other research methods

Aga Khan Foundation *Rapid Participatory Rural Appraisal. Frontiers of Research*
AKF, 33 Thurloe Square, London, October 1991, 130 pages

Chambers, R. *Putting The Last, First,* Longman 1983

Chambers, R *PRA Notes:* available from IIED, London.

Clark University, Programme for International Development, *Implementing PRA: A Handbook to Facilitate Participatory Rural Appraisal,* March 1992.
(This and other publications available from Program for International Development, Clark University, 950 main Street, Worcester, MA 01540-1477, USA. free to agencies working in the same field.)

Grandin, B E. *Wealth Ranking in Smallholder Communities: A Field Manual*
Intermediate Technology Publications, 1988, 49 pp.

Gueye B and Schoonmaker-Freudenberger K *Introduction a la methode accelere de recherche participative (MARP); quelques notes pour appuyer une formation pratique,* London IIED, 1991.

Guijt, I; (ed) *Tecnicas de comunicacao para extensionistas; relatorio de um seminario em diagnostico rural (rapido) participativo.* SARDEP/IIED, 1991.
(Portuguese language — report of a seminar on PRA techniques available from IIED., 3 Endsleigh Street, London WC1H 0DD.)

Nichols, P. *Social Survey Methods: A Fieldguide for Development Workers,* Oxfam Development Guidelines Series No. 6
Oxfam, Oxford, 1991, 130 pp

Pratt, B. Loizos, P. *Choosing Research Methods: Data Collection for Development Workers,* Oxfam Development Guidelines Series No. 7
Oxfam, Oxford, 1992, 128 pp

RRA Notes Series available from IIED, London.
These are regular collections of individual researcher's, practitioner's, or group's experiences with RRA and PRA.

Theis, J. and Grady, H.M. *Participatory Rapid Appraisal for Community Development.*

Index

Oxfam Books

Oxfam publishes a wide range of books, manuals, and resources for specialists, academics, teachers, and general readers. For a free catalogue, write to: Oxfam Publishing, Oxfam, 274 Banbury Road, Oxford OX2 7DZ, UK.

Basic Accounting for Small Groups
John Cammack

A step-by-step guide to basic accounting and financial management techniques for those with no previous experience of accounting and book-keeping. This book is ideal for any small group which needs to keep accurate records of its financial transactions.

085598 148 2 illustrated

The Financial Management of a Small Handicraft Business
Edward Millard

This guide explains the basic financial concepts involved in the effective planning of day-to-day operations which will help businesses to calculate working capital requirements and achieve profitability.

0 85598 082 6 illustrated

Export Marketing for a Small Handicraft Business
Edward Millard

Written in clear and accessible language with the small handicraft producer firmly in mind, this helpful book covers such issues as market research, contact with customers, product development and design, packaging, and export formalities.

0 85598 174 1 illustrated

Evaluating Social Development Projects

Edited by Peter Oakley and David Marsden

The goals of many social development programmes involve issues such as the development of indigenous sustainable capacity, the promotion of participation, the awakening of consciousness, and the encouragement of self-reliant strategies. Looking in detail at these aims, this book addresses such questions as: how are these achievements to be measured? What are the purposes of evaluations of these sorts of projects? Are evaluations of such projects essentially different from those of more conventional infrastructural projects?

0 85598 146 6 hardback
0 85598 147 4 paperback

Behind the Lines of Stone
The Social Impact of a Soil and Water Conservation Project in the Sahel

Nicholas Atampugre

Oxfam's experimental soil and water conservation in the drought-prone Yatenga region of Burkina Faso won international acclaim and many imitators. The innovative techniques resulted in significantly increased cereal yields, and natural vegetation began to grow spontaneously again.

Oxfam commissioned a survey to discover how the project had affected the poorest in the community, especially women. The findings form the basis of this book, which will be of great interest to those involved in agricultural and environmental programmes, as well as community development workers in the field, and academics concerned with agricultural development in arid climates.

0 85598 257 8 hardback
0 85598 258 6 paperback